MACHINES ★ AT WORK

AMBULANCES

BY GARY M. AMOROSO AND CYNTHIA A. KLINGEL

THE CHILD'S WORLD® • MANKATO, MINNESOTA

The Child's® World

Published in the United States of America by The Child's World®
1980 Lookout Drive • Mankato, MN 56003-1705
800-599-READ • www.childsworld.com

PHOTO CREDITS
© Corbis: 19
© David M. Budd Photography: cover, 2, 4, 8 (main), 11, 12, 15
© iStockphoto.com/Loic Bernard: 7
© iStockphoto.com/Nancy Louie: 16
© iStockphoto.com/Nicky Blade: 3
© iStockphoto.com/Scott Fichter: 8 (inset)
© Stephen Coburn/BigStockPhoto.com: 20

ACKNOWLEDGMENTS
The Child's World®: Mary Berendes, Publishing Director;
Katherine Stevenson, Editor

The Design Lab: Kathleen Petelinsek, Design and Page Production

9/08

LIBRARY OF CONGRESS CATALOGING-IN-PUBLICATION DATA
Amoroso, Gary M.
  Ambulances / by Gary M. Amoroso and Cynthia A. Klingel.
      p. cm.
  Includes bibliographical references and index.
  ISBN 1-59296-826-0 (library bound : alk. paper)
  1. Ambulances—Juvenile literature. 2. Ambulance service—Juvenile literature.
I. Klingel, Cynthia Fitterer. II. Title.
  TL235.8.A46 2006
  629.222'34—dc22   2006023278

c!

⭐ Contents

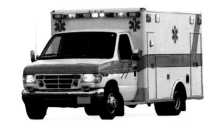

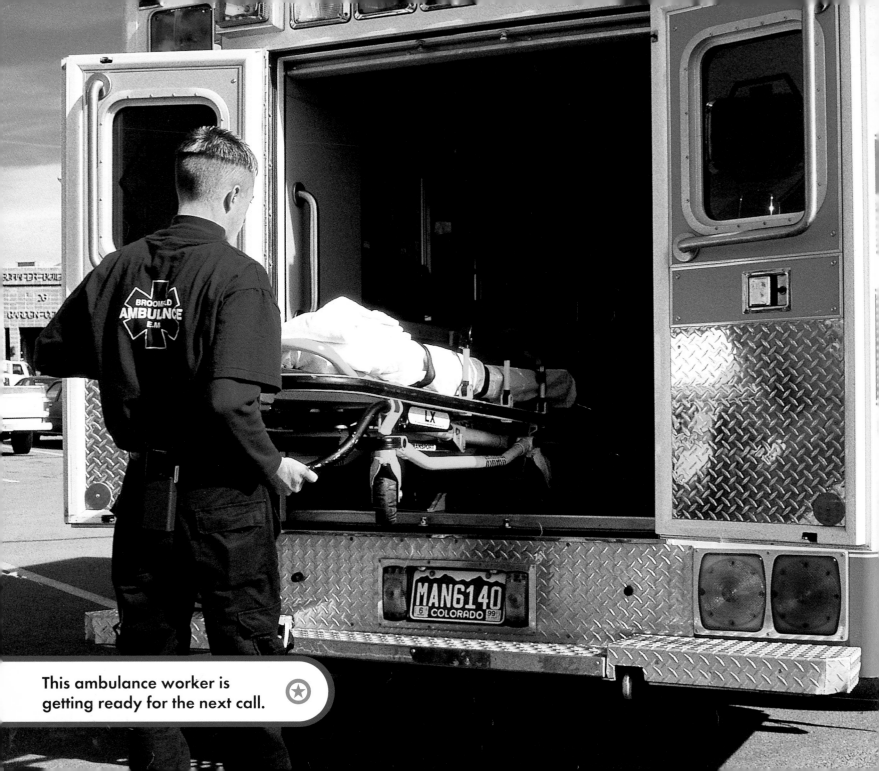

This ambulance worker is getting ready for the next call.

What are ambulances?

Ambulances are special types of **vehicles**. They carry people who are sick or hurt. They take the people to **hospitals**.

5

When are ambulances used?

Ambulances are used in **emergencies**. They are used when people are **injured** or get very ill. They are used after car crashes or fires. They are used when people need to get to a doctor—fast!

6

This ambulance is on its way to a hospital.
You often see ambulances on city streets.

siren ⟹

The sirens are on the front of the ambulance. The lights are on both the front and the back. They are red, yellow, blue, and white. ⊛

What do ambulances look like?

Most ambulances look like trucks or vans. But they have special markings and lettering. They have bright flashing lights. They have loud **sirens** and horns. The lights and noise tell other drivers that an ambulance is coming.

9

What is inside an ambulance?

Inside, an ambulance is set up for helping people. The people who need help are called **patients**. A **stretcher** keeps the patient safe and still.

10

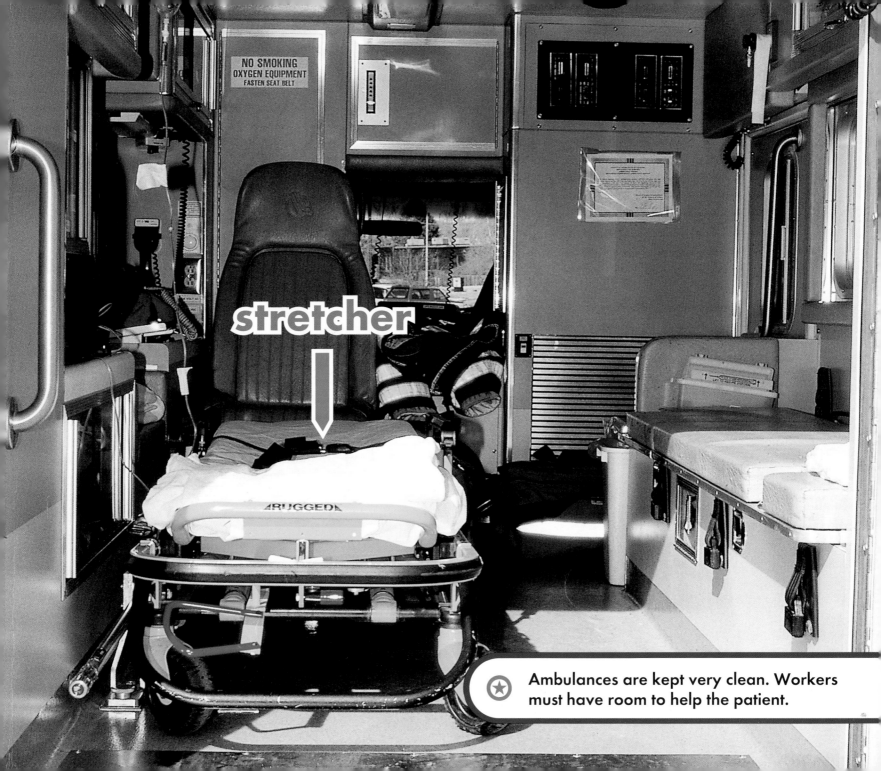

stretcher

Ambulances are kept very clean. Workers must have room to help the patient.

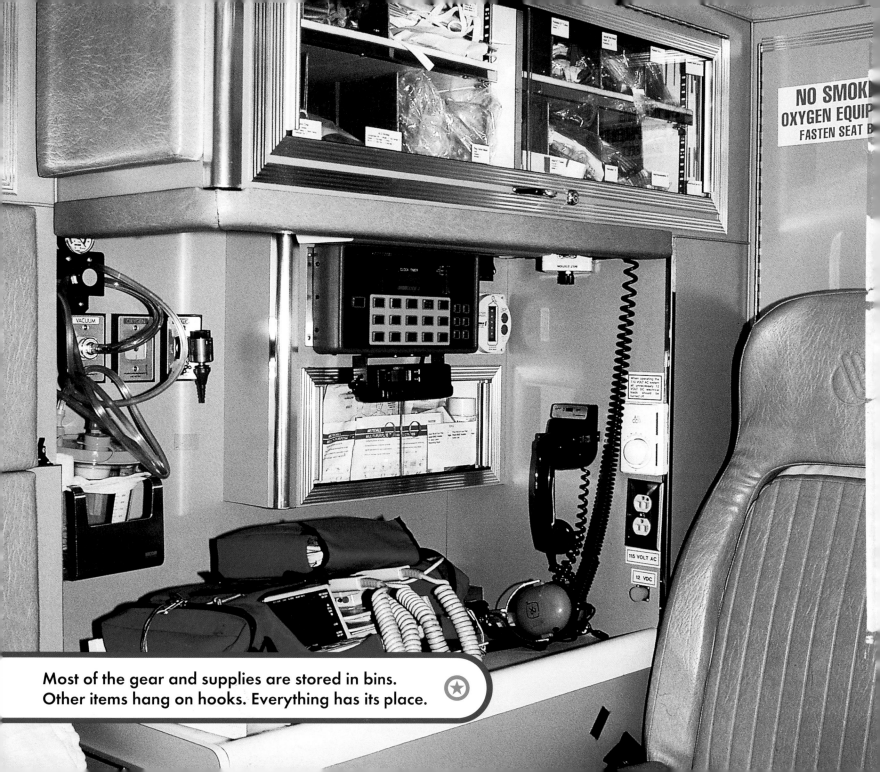

Most of the gear and supplies are stored in bins.
Other items hang on hooks. Everything has its place.

 The ambulance carries lots of gear and supplies. They help the ambulance workers take care of the patient.

13

 # Who works in ambulances?

One person drives the ambulance. At least one other worker rides with the patient. The patient gets help even while the ambulance is moving.

14

bench

⬇

⭐ The second worker sits near the patient. Sometimes a family member rides along, too. The family member sits on a small bench.

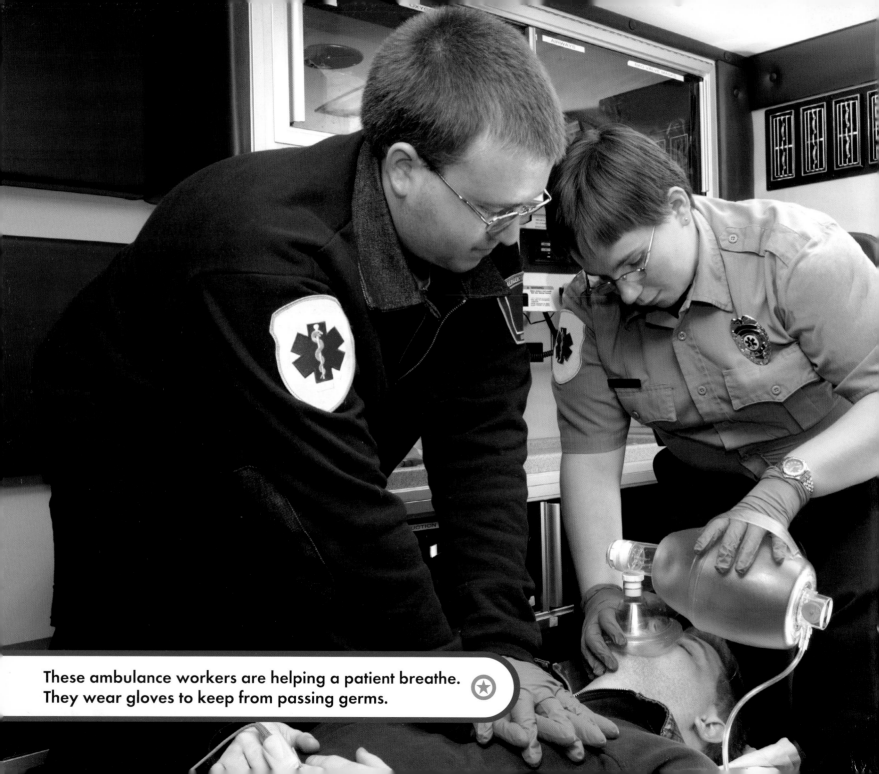

These ambulance workers are helping a patient breathe.
They wear gloves to keep from passing germs.

There are different kinds of ambulance workers. All of them are specially trained for the job. They know how to take care of many illnesses and injuries.

What happens inside ambulances?

Ambulance workers start helping patients right away. They help stop bleeding. They help patients breathe. They help with broken bones or other injuries. They keep patients safe until they get to the hospital.

18

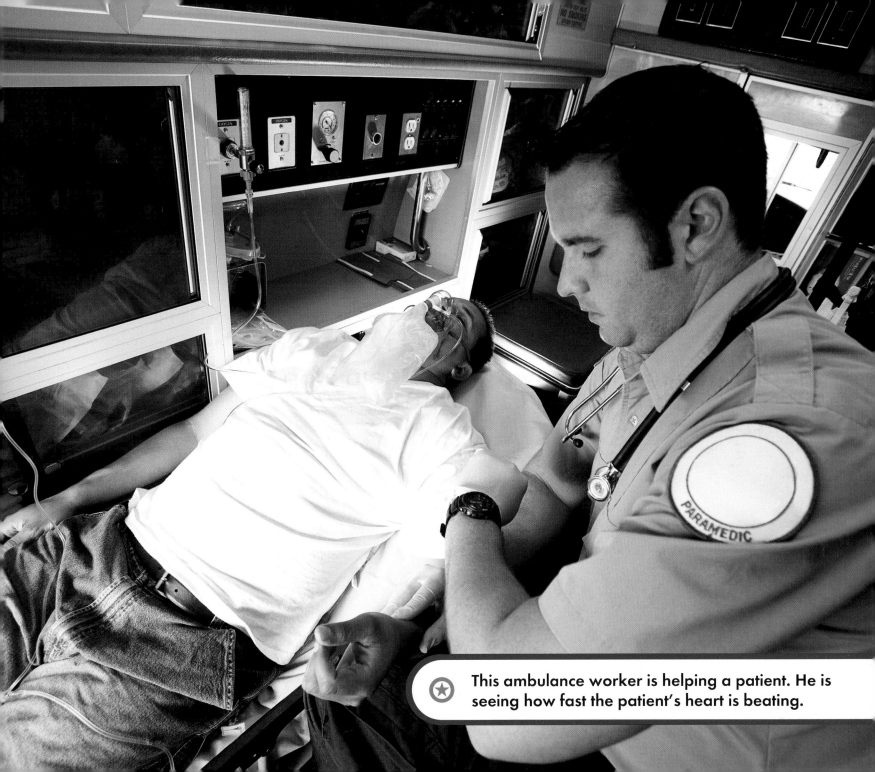

This ambulance worker is helping a patient. He is seeing how fast the patient's heart is beating.

This ambulance is racing down the street. Other cars must pull over to let it pass.

Are ambulances important?

Ambulances are used all over the world. They help out in all kinds of emergencies. They save many lives every day. Ambulances are very important!

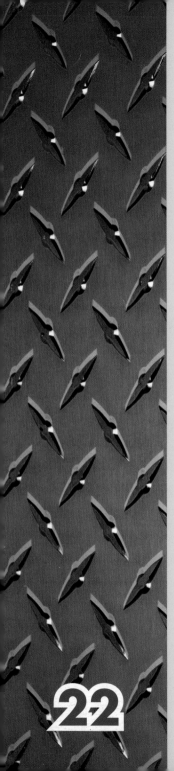

 # Glossary

emergencies (ih-MUR-junt-seez) Emergencies are times of danger, when people must act quickly.

hospitals (HOSS-pih-tulz) Hospitals are places that take care of sick or injured people.

injured (IN-jurd) To get injured is to get hurt.

patients (PAY-shuntz) Patients are people who are getting help for a health problem.

sirens (SY-runz) Sirens make loud noises to let people know there is danger.

stretcher (STREH-chur) A stretcher is a bed used to carry people who are ill or hurt.

vehicles (VEE-uh-kullz) Vehicles are things for carrying people or goods.

 # Books

Ethan, Eric. *Ambulances.* Milwaukee, WI: Gareth Stevens, 2002.

Levine, Michelle. *Ambulances.* Minneapolis, MN: Lerner Publications, 2004.

Teitelbaum, Michael, Isidre Mones (illustrator), and Marc Mones (illustrator). *If I Could Drive an Ambulance!* New York: Scholastic, 2003.

 # Web Sites

Visit our Web site for lots of links about ambulances:
http://www.childsworld.com/links

Note to parents, teachers, and librarians: We routinely check our Web links to make sure they're safe, active sites—so encourage your readers to check them out!

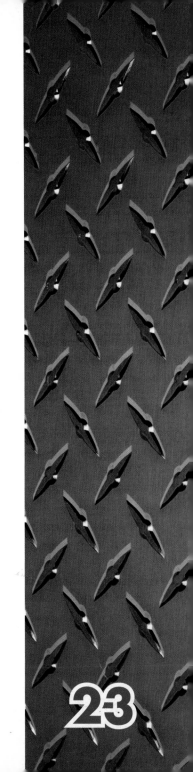

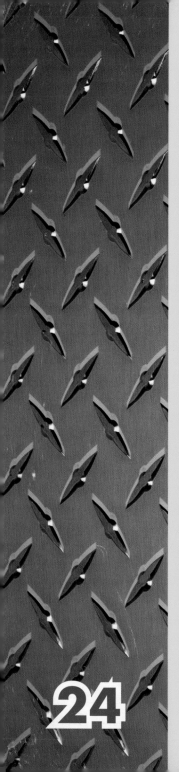

 # Index

 # About the Author

Gary M. Amoroso lives in Minnesota and enjoys traveling, sports, and having fun with friends and family. He has been a coach, teacher, principal, and district superintendent.

Cynthia A. Klingel is a Director of Curriculum and Instruction in a Minnesota school district. She enjoys reading, writing, gardening, traveling, and spending time with friends and family.